My Show Day

My Favourite Day

Dear Mom and Dad,

Dear Mom and Dad,

We went to the show.

Dear Mom and Dad,
We went to the show.

We looked at the sheep.

Dear Mom and Dad,
   We went to the show.
We looked at the sheep.

We looked at the chicks.

Dear Mom and Dad,
We went to the show.
We looked at the sheep.
We looked at the chicks.

We played a game.
Nana helped me
throw the ball.

Dear Mom and Dad,
  We went to the show.
We looked at the sheep.
  We looked at the chicks.
We played a game.
Nana helped me
throw the ball.

I had some fairy floss.

Dear Mom and Dad,
  We went to the show.
We looked at the sheep.
  We looked at the chicks.
We played a game.
Nana helped me
throw the ball.
I had some fairy floss.

We looked at the fireworks.

Dear Mom and Dad,

We went to the show.

We looked at the sheep.

We looked at the chicks.

We played a game.

Nana helped me
throw the ball.

I had some fairy floss.

We looked at the fireworks.

Dear Mom and Dad,
  We went to the show.
We looked at the sheep.
  We looked at the chicks.
We played a game.
Nana helped me
throw the ball.
I had some fairy floss.
We looked at the fireworks.
  I liked going to the show.
Love from Sam.